21st Century Skills Library

REAL WORLD MATH: PERSONAL FINANCE

UNDERSTANDING TAXES

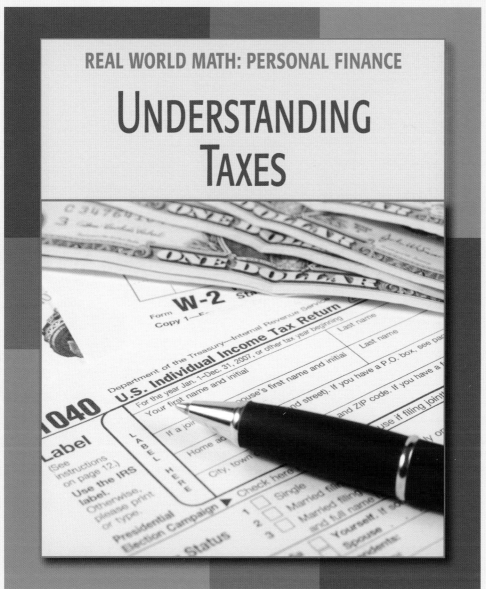

Cecilia Minden

Cherry Lake Publishing
Ann Arbor, Michigan

Published in the United States of America by Cherry Lake Publishing
Ann Arbor, Michigan
www.cherrylakepublishing.com

Math Education Adviser: Tonya Walker, Boston University

Finance Adviser: Jill Klooster, CPA, Kitchenmaster & Company

Photo Credits: Cover and page 1, ©Dmitry Melnikov, used under license
from Shutterstock, Inc.; page 4, ©North Wind Picture Archives/Alamy; page 8,
©Lawrence Wee, used under license from Shutterstock, Inc.; page 10, ©Orange
Line Media, used under license from Shutterstock, Inc.; page 14, ©Blend Images/
Alamy; page 16, ©Image Source Pink/Alamy; page 19, ©GoGo Images Corporation/
Alamy; page 20, ©Jupiterimages/Comstock Images; page 24, ©Picture Contact/Alamy;
page 26, ©Jaimie Duplass, used under license from Shutterstock, Inc.

Library of Congress Cataloging-in-Publication Data
Minden, Cecilia.
 Understanding taxes / Cecilia Minden.
 p. cm.—(Real world math)
Includes index.
ISBN-13: 978-1-60279-311-8
ISBN-10: 1-60279-311-5
1. Taxation—United States—Juvenile literature. 2. Taxation—Juvenile
literature. I. Title.
HJ2381.M48 2009
336.200973—dc22   2008025513

Cherry Lake Publishing would like to acknowledge the work of
The Partnership for 21st Century Skills.
Please visit www.21stcenturyskills.org for more information.

TABLE OF CONTENTS

CHAPTER ONE

TAXES IN THE UNITED STATES

During the Boston Tea Party, colonists dumped more than 300 chests of tea into Boston Harbor. This was done to protest taxes they thought were unfair.

On a dark night in 1773, approximately 200 men dressed as Native

Americans met near Boston Harbor. They marched toward three cargo

ships docked at Griffin's Wharf.

England was fighting a war with France. It needed money to pay the expenses. Tea was an important part of colonial life. England thought the colonists would be willing to pay higher taxes to get their tea. But instead of paying these taxes, the angry colonists dumped the tea into the harbor. Their actions eventually led to the American Revolution.

REAL WORLD MATH CHALLENGE

During the Civil War, Congress passed the Revenue Act of 1861. People who earned $800 a year or more had to pay 3% of their income in taxes to the government. Nathan Healy earned $967 in 1862. **How much did Nathan pay in taxes? How much money did Nathan have left after he paid his taxes?**

(Turn to page 29 for the answers)

Just as in colonial times, taxes continue to support the government. The U.S. Constitution grants power to the **federal** government to collect taxes. Congress determines how tax money is spent. We vote for people to represent us in Congress. We trust them to make good judgments about how our tax money is spent.

Taxes support three types of government: federal, state, and local. Our federal government is responsible for protecting and serving all 50 states and the District of Columbia. More than 300 million people live in the United States. It takes a lot of money to care for the needs of each citizen. State governments pay for many of our needs, including state roads.

Every state is divided into smaller sections. These sections are called counties or parishes. Local government includes both city and county government. The money people pay in local income tax is often used to fund local projects such as public schools.

Canada's tax system is similar to the U.S. system.

Instead of states, Canada is divided into provinces

and territories. Each province collects taxes to care

for the needs of its citizens.

Our taxes are not used just to support the

government. Using our math skills, we will learn

about how tax dollars provide you with many of the

things you need and use every day.

Not paying your taxes is against the law. Sometimes people refuse to pay taxes for specific reasons. They don't want their money to support a certain project or idea. Some might refuse to pay taxes that support a war. Others may refuse to pay taxes that fund projects that harm the environment. In the end, they still have to pay taxes. But by protesting, they are also able to draw attention to their beliefs.

The most effective protestors are able to clearly and peacefully communicate their ideas to get their message across. Do you think a person should ever break a law to support an idea he or she feels strongly about?

CHAPTER TWO

WHERE DOES TAX MONEY GO?

Imagine what a street would look like if no one repaired the damage caused by bad weather or everyday use. Taxes help support street maintenance.

Let's go through an average day to see how many of the things we use

involve tax dollars in some way. What's the first thing you do when you

wake up? Do you brush your teeth or take a shower? Companies that provide services such as water have to follow local and state guidelines. The guidelines ensure that your water is safe for you to use. Your tax dollars pay inspectors to enforce these guidelines.

Next, you probably eat breakfast. The job of the U.S. Food and Drug Administration (FDA) is to protect and promote your health. The organization makes sure that many types of food and medicine are safe.

Do you ride a public bus to school? Tax dollars also pay for transportation. Do you attend a public school? All three types of government support public schools. Look around your school. Many things were paid for with tax dollars. That includes the school building itself and the playground equipment.

After school, do you spend time at a local park? Are there playing fields and places to sit? Maybe you like going to the library. Do you ride your

Tax dollars may be used to train firefighters and run fire departments. In this way, your tax money can help save lives.

bike on city streets? Parks, libraries, and city streets all rely on tax dollars that are spent in your community. Taxes also help support the police and fire departments, as well as health care. Sometimes taxes pay for workers to pick up and recycle your trash.

State governments support state highways and bridges. They maintain state parks and wildlife. Taxes are used to maintain lakes, rivers, and shorelines. State governments also support

some colleges and universities.

Taxes at the federal level support our

military forces at home and overseas. Taxes help

fund space exploration. The federal government

also pays for interstate highways. Tax dollars

support national parks such as Grand Canyon

and Yellowstone. Perhaps you've seen the Statue

of Liberty. Sites such as this one are important

to the history of our nation. They are all

maintained in part by tax dollars.

All over the world, citizens pay taxes to help

support their governments. In Canada, taxes

21st Century Content

Imagine losing your home in a flood, hurricane, earthquake, or tornado. An important use of federal tax dollars is to help people in need. When a disaster strikes, a state's governor requests help from the federal government. If the president declares a state of emergency, victims can seek help from the Federal Emergency Management Agency (FEMA). Officials and volunteers work together to provide food, water, and shelter for those affected by the disaster.

In order to work effectively together, people must cooperate and be flexible during difficult situations. After all, everyone shares the common goal of helping disaster victims. Has there been a natural disaster in your state? How did your government respond?

support many programs including health care, public safety, and help for farmers.

Every office of the government receives money from **tax revenues**. Each office creates budgets to help manage how the money is spent. The federal government also sets aside money in the form of **grants** and **loans**. Loans need to be repaid, but grants do not. Many people are able to attend college using federal grants and loans. Once students have graduated, they begin paying back loans. This makes sure there will be money for the next

REAL WORLD MATH CHALLENGE

Asheville has enough tax revenue to budget $34 million for education. The town has 9 elementary schools, 2 middle schools, and 1 high school. Within the education budget, 65% is for instruction. **How much money will go to instruction? If each school receives an equal amount, how much money will each school receive for instruction?**

(Turn to page 29 for the answers)

group of students to go to school. Researchers receive grant money for many reasons, including studying how to cure diseases.

Our tax money isn't used just to help people in our own country. The United States also sends tax money to other nations to help in a variety of ways. Sometimes the money is for disaster relief. Other times it is used to help countries build schools or hospitals.

Other countries help as well. In 2008, Canada created the Sichuan Earthquake Relief Fund. It was designed to help Chinese earthquake victims.

Supporting all these programs takes trillions of tax dollars. So where does all the tax money come from? Two primary sources of tax revenue are sales tax and income tax. Let's use our math skills to learn how each of these is calculated.

CHAPTER THREE

DO THE MATH: SALES TAX

*You pay the same amount of sales tax whether you use
cash or a credit card to make a purchase.*

England taxed the colonists on tea because government leaders knew

it was an item in high demand. Taxes are still based on demand. We are

willing to pay sales tax on items because they are things we need or want.

There isn't a national sales tax in the United States. Leaders of each

state determine how much sales tax will be charged. Not all states have a sales tax. Alaska, Delaware, Montana, New Hampshire, and Oregon do not charge a sales tax. Other states charge a single tax rate on all purchased goods. Some of these states include Connecticut, Hawaii, Indiana, Kentucky, Maine, Maryland, Massachusetts, Michigan, Mississippi, New Jersey, Rhode Island, and Vermont.

There are exceptions with most states. Massachusetts, for example, doesn't charge sales tax on clothing or shoes that cost less that $175. Minnesota doesn't charge a sales tax on food unless it is prepared food.

REAL WORLD MATH CHALLENGE

Lupita is shopping for school supplies. She buys a box of pens for $2.29, some paper for $6.75, and a 3-ring binder for $3.98. She also buys a school sweater for $23.98. Lupita's state charges a 3% sales tax on clothing. There is an 8% sales tax on all other items. **How much did Lupita pay in sales tax? What is the total amount of her purchase?**

(Turn to page 29 for the answers)

If you can't find the amount of tax you were charged on the receipt, a store employee will be happy to help. Just ask!

Sales tax is charged at the point of sale. This means you do not owe any tax unless you purchase the item. The store is responsible for passing the tax money on to the government. Sales tax is a percentage of your total purchase. It is important to consider the tax when determining if you have enough money for your purchases.

For example, you have $55 to spend on a coat. You find one for $51.75. Don't forget that there is also a 4.5% sales tax. Do you have enough?

A quick way to estimate your total purchase is by rounding off. Round $51.75 up to $52.00. Round 4.5% up to 5%. Do a quick calculation of the sales tax: $0.05 \times \$52 = \$2.60$. Now estimate your total: $\$2.60 + \$52 = \$54.60$. By coming up with a rough estimate, you were able to figure out that you had enough money to buy your coat.

The sales tax is not listed on the sales tag. It should be on your receipt. The percentage and the amount of sales tax are listed near the total. This will tell you exactly how much sales tax you've paid on your items.

Canada also charges sales tax. Their federal tax is called a goods and services tax (GST). Most provinces have a provincial sales tax (PST) on a variety of goods and services. In some provinces, the GST and PST are combined to create a harmonized sales tax (HST). That way, citizens pay one tax rate.

21st Century Content

Every August, many states declare a sales tax holiday. It usually lasts for one weekend. No taxes are charged on things students will need for school. Specific items vary per state, but they might include certain clothing and shoes priced under $100.

A sales tax holiday is a great chance for students to take advantage of special rates. It is important for students to be aware of opportunities such as this one because it can save them money on purchases. Making a list of items you need and comparing sale prices will also help you make smart economic choices. Where could you find out if your state has a sales tax holiday?

Goods grown or manufactured in the United States provide jobs for many people. To discourage people from purchasing products from other countries, a high tax is placed on imported goods. This is called a tariff or a duty tax.

A luxury tax is placed on items that are not considered **essential** to our lives. Products that may have a luxury tax include expensive cars and jewelry. A sin tax is placed on certain items. The idea is that by charging a high tax on products that are harmful, people will purchase less of those products. Sin taxes are often charged on alcohol and tobacco products.

Many families own at least one car. Do you think luxury taxes affect the types of cars people are willing to buy?

Sales taxes help cover some of the cost of many of the services listed in the previous chapter. You need an income, however, to go shopping. And when you make that income, you will be—you guessed it—taxed!

CHAPTER FOUR

Do the Math: Income Tax

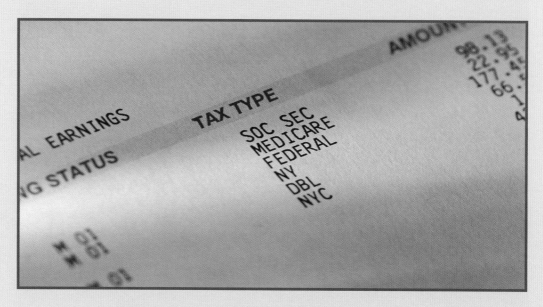

Each earnings statement lists the type and amount of tax that gets deducted from your income. Save this information for your records.

Math skills can help you understand how income taxes work. In the previous chapter you learned about sales tax. But sales tax pays for only some of the government's expenses. Income tax helps cover the rest.

Most people pay taxes all year long. When you look at a paycheck, you will see deductions for federal income tax, state income tax, and FICA tax.

FICA stands for Federal Insurance Contributions Act. This tax pays for

Social Security benefits and Medicare.

Do you have a Social Security number? The U.S. government uses this

number to keep track of each citizen. People pay a percentage of their income

in the form of Social Security taxes. This money is used to help support a

variety of people. Some groups who can collect Social Security money include

retired and disabled people. The original age for full retirement was 65. The

age is gradually being changed to 67 for full retirement. The amount of money

you receive from Social Security is based on money you made while you were

working. The Social Security system helps people pay for living expenses when

they can no longer earn a salary. Medicare is a type of health insurance system.

It helps cover the cost of medical expenses for people age 65 and older. It also

helps seriously disabled people.

Employees are not the only ones who pay taxes. Some taxes that most employers pay include federal and state unemployment taxes. This money is for people who lose their jobs. They can receive money from the government to help pay bills until they find other jobs.

Canada has a similar system for collecting and distributing taxes. The Canada Revenue Agency (CRA) manages the tax system. Citizens contribute to the Canada Pension Plan (CPP). In part, the program provides income for people who are no longer able to work. The

REAL WORLD MATH CHALLENGE

Emani has an after-school job at a fast-food restaurant. He makes $7.00 an hour. Last week he worked 13 hours. He was surprised to find that 33% of his check was deducted for federal, state, and FICA taxes. **How much money did Emani have left after paying taxes?**

(Turn to page 29 for the answer)

Employment Insurance program provides income for the unemployed.

Most U.S. citizens must pay their federal income tax by April 15 each year. Federal tax forms are filed with the Internal Revenue Service (IRS). The IRS determines how much federal tax you should've paid in the previous year based on your gross income. Gross income is all the money you earned from January 1 to December 31 of the previous year. States that tax income generally use this same figure to determine your state income tax. There are many federal and state laws that govern taxes.

Many people prepare their own tax forms and figure out what they must pay. But some people use the services of tax accountants and tax attorneys. Tax accountants help make sure that taxes are filed accurately. Tax attorneys specialize in handling legal problems between taxpayers and the IRS or other organizations.

People depend on tax accountants and attorneys to handle important information. Any mistakes could result in fines or even jail time for a taxpayer. To keep up with changes in rules and tax laws, many lawyers and accountants attend classes throughout their career. They know that learning is a lifelong process. Can you think of another career in which people take classes to keep up with the latest information?

Donations to many charitable organizations are tax deductible. UNICEF is one such organization that provides help to children around the world.

In Canada, people have about two extra weeks. Their deadline is

April 30.

The government knows that each person has different needs. To help

people take care of those needs, the government allows for tax deductions.

A tax deduction is money that is subtracted from your gross income.

The idea is that you are lowering the amount of income that is being taxed.

You end up paying less in taxes. There are many cases in which people

use tax deductions. An example would be when you are responsible for

another person. Parents take tax deductions for each of their **dependent**

children. The amount left over is called your adjusted gross income

(AGI). This is the amount used to determine your taxes. If you've paid too

much tax during the year, you will receive a tax refund. You will receive a

payment from the government.

Sales tax and income tax provide money that our government uses

to pay for public services. There are other taxes as well. U.S. citizens

pay property taxes. Property may include cars, boats, houses, and other

building structures. We also pay taxes on home **utilities** such as electricity,

gas, and water. We pay a fuel tax when we buy gasoline.

CHAPTER FIVE

MAKE YOUR TAXES WORK FOR YOU

Some libraries offer wireless Internet connections in addition to shared computer stations. This is useful for people who bring their own laptops. Tax dollars pay for this service.

There are several ways to get the most for your tax dollar. One of them is

to take advantage of all the government programs supported by tax dollars.

Many people don't realize all the services available at a public library. Tax

dollars pay for millions of books each year. Libraries also have magazines,

CDs, and DVDs that you can borrow, usually for free. All you need is a library card. Most public libraries also have

computer stations that provide free Internet access.

Sometimes the government will use tax

money to help fund a special celebration.

In 2008, Canadians enjoyed Democracy 250.

This series of events was designed to celebrate

250 years of democracy in the nation. There were

concerts and other special events funded by the

government for people to enjoy.

You can have a lot of fun visiting institutions

that are supported by tax dollars. For example,

admission is free for the zoo and all Smithsonian

museums in Washington, DC.

21st Century Content

Stay informed. When you hear about a new tax law, try to understand how it could affect you and your family. Taxes are meant to serve the common good. This means that all citizens should benefit from tax dollars. It would not be fair to pass a tax that would not help many people. We elect others to political positions to defend our rights. During elections, listen to what candidates have to say about their beliefs. Support people who share your beliefs. These men and women play a part in passing laws that will make a difference in our lives. This includes laws involving taxes.

Being an informed citizen will help you understand why people pay taxes and how that tax revenue is used.

REAL WORLD MATH CHALLENGE

Springfield budgeted $350,000 for improvements for local parks. The entire town budget was $3.4 million. **What percentage was spent on local parks?** Round your answer to the nearest whole percent.
(Turn to page 29 for the answer)

If you have Internet access, you can take advantage of the many Web sites funded by tax dollars. Some day you may go to college. Consider applying for grants and loans from the government to help cover college expenses.

You pay sales tax. When you have a job, you will begin to pay other taxes. Not paying taxes is against the law. Without taxes, the government would not have enough income for all the services it provides.

Now, use your math skills to count all the ways you can make your tax dollars work for you!

REAL WORLD MATH CHALLENGE ANSWERS

Chapter One
Page 5

Nathan paid $29.01 in taxes.

$967 x 0.03 = $29.01

He had $937.99 left over after taxes.

$967 – $29.01 = $937.99

Chapter Two
Page 12

Asheville will budget $22,100,000 for instruction.

$34,000,000 x 0.65 = $22,100,000

There are 12 schools.

9 + 2 + 1 = 12

Each school will receive $1,841,666.67 for instruction.

$22,100,000 / 12 = $1,841,666.666 =
$1,841,666.67

Chapter Three
Page 15

Lupita spent $1.04 in taxes on supplies.

$2.29 + $6.75 + $3.98 = $13.02

$13.02 x 0.08 = 1.0416 = $1.04

She spent $0.72 in taxes on the sweater.

$23.98 x 0.03 = 0.7194 = $0.72

She spent a total of $1.76 in sales tax.

$1.04 + $0.72 = $1.76

Her total purchase was $38.76

$13.02 + $1.04 + $23.98 + $0.72 = $38.76

Chapter Four
Page 22

Emani's gross income was $91.00.

$7.00 x 13 = $91.00

He paid $30.03 in taxes.

$91 x 0.33 = $30.03

The amount of his paycheck was $60.97

$91 – $30.03 = $60.97

Chapter Five
Page 28

Springfield spent approximately 10% of the total budget on improvements for local parks.

$350,000 ÷ $3,400,000 = 0.102 = 10%

Glossary

deductions (di-DUHK-shuhnz) amounts that are subtracted from a larger amount

dependent (di-PEN-duhnt) relying on another person

essential (i-SEN-shuhl) very important

federal (FED-ur-uhl) related to a central government or authority

grants (grantss) amounts of money awarded by the government for a specific purpose

loans (lohnz) things that are borrowed, especially money

tax revenues (taks REV-uh-nooz) income from taxes

utilities (yoo-TIL-uh-teez) basic services such as electricity and water

FOR MORE INFORMATION

Books

Bedesky, Baron. *What Are Taxes?* New York: Crabtree Publishing, 2009.

Friedman, Mark. *Government: How Local, State, and Federal Government Works.* Chanhassen, MN: The Child's World, 2005.

Kowalski, Kathiann M., *Taxes.* Tarrytown, NY: Benchmark Books, 2006.

Web Sites

FEMA for Kids: About the Agency
www.fema.gov/kids/about1.htm
Find out more about one organization that is funded by tax dollars

Northwestern Mutual Foundation: Decoding Your Paycheck
www.themint.org/kids/decoding-your-paycheck.html
Check out a sample earnings statement and see what gets deducted from a paycheck

The Official Kids' Portal for the U.S. Government
www.kids.gov/
Learn more about the Social Security system and other government programs

INDEX

ABOUT THE AUTHOR

Cecilia Minden, PhD, is a former classroom teacher and university professor. She now enjoys working as a literacy consultant and writer for school and library publications. She has written more than 50 books for children. Cecilia lives with her family near Chapel Hill, North Carolina.